How to Think in English in Three Vital Steps

HELP YOUR ESL/EFL STUDENTS JOIN THE GLOBAL COMMUNITY

Leona Wellington, M.Ed.
Global EFL/ESL Teacher-Trainer

Published by Bonsai Blue Publications
27 Fitzgerald St. Wentworth Falls,
Blue Mountains, Australia NSW 2782

DISCLAIMER:

This book, along with any claims, opinions or suggestions is not based on empirical research which the author didn't have the time or resources for. Instead she did action research to test out what was working or not working. It wasn't until years later that she was able to validate the correctness or incorrectness of what she had done.

As far as she knows, ESL/EFL is not usually viewed or approached in the same manner in which she is suggesting. Her aim is to set the groundwork or a template that students will need to acquire a structural foundation of English.

It is not within the scope of this book to interpret semantic or implied variations of vocabulary words themselves. Instead it focuses on the templates that comprise the basic components of English and define its core mechanics. These are the ones needed to think in English. How vocabulary affects meaning is not the main objective of this book. It is just frosting on the cake.

She does not claim to have all the answers but bases her opinions on personal experience in language acquisition, observation of English in general and ESL/EFL in particular as well as the excellent results she has obtained from teaching English according to what she now considers the five major building blocks and essential tools of the language.

How to Think in English, is the first of these building blocks and vital for acquiring the language.

Table of Contents

WHY I WROTE THIS BOOK 5

HOW CAN THIS BOOK HELP YOU? 7

ENDORSEMENTS 8

INTRODUCTION 11
    THE 'AHA' MOMENT 11
    THE THREE SLOTS 12
    DID IT SINK IN? 14
    SVO CAN SHOCK ADVANCED STUDENTS 15

CHAPTER I 16

THE THREE BROTHERS LAW 16
    WHAT IS SVO? 17
    SLOT 1 (NOUN PHRASE) 17
    EIGHT ASPECTS OF 'S' IN SVO: 17

A NOUN IS A NOUN IS A NOUN..18
    THE FIRST BROTHER: 20
    SENTENCES DRESS DIFFERENTLY 21
    THE LAZIEST PRIMA DONNAS EVER 22

MAJOR TYPES OF SENTENCES 24
    USING A TRANSITIVE VERB 24
    USING LINKING AND INTRANSITIVE VERBS.......................... 25
    SV ALONE OR WITH COMPLIMENT 27

SUBJECT PRONOUNS 29
    THE SEVEN DIPLOMATS 29
    BUT IS IT A SUBJECT OR OBJECT? 31

MULTITASKING OUTSIDE OF SVO 32
    THE GREAT IMPOSTOR PRONOUNS...................................... 32
    PRONOUNS AS EXTRA FROSTING 33
    PRONOUNS AS GREAT IMPOSTORS 33

ACTIVITY 35
    THE BIG PRONOUN GIVEAWAY: 35
    EXTENSION ONE—SOME FROSTING 37
    EXTENSION TWO—RETURN TO OWNER 38

ADDITIONAL ACTIVITY CONSIDERATIONS **42**
OBJECTS HAVE TWO FACES *42*

CHAPTER II **47**
SLOT 2 (VERB PHRASE) *47*

BUT THERE ARE THOUSANDS OF VERBS! **47**
THE HUB OR STAR OF THE SHOW *47*
HOW TO GET ALONG WITH THE STAR *48*

CHAPTER III **52**
SLOT 3 (OBJECT/COMPLEMENT) *52*

THERE'S A BLACK SHEEP IN EVERY FAMILY **52**
WHY DO WE NEGLECT THE OBVIOUS? *56*
'NAME YOUR SUBJECT' *58*

SVO IN RELATION TO CULTURE? **60**

HOW DO I START THE ACTION? **63**
YOU 'GOTTA' NAIL DOWN THE NOUN *63*

ACTIVITY **64**
BUILD THE WILDEST SUBJECT *64*
ABOUT DETERMINERS *66*

SHALL WE BUILD A MONSTER? **68**
STOP HERE OR WALK ON THE WILD SIDE *71*
THE ACCORDION PRINCIPLE *75*
SUBJECTS CAN BE OBJECTS: *78*

ENGAGING THE RIGHT BRAIN **80**
LEAN HEAVILY ON THE RIGHT *81*

STRATEGIES FOR ALL LEVELS **82**

ACHIEVEMENTS AND PITFALLS **86**

HOW TO THINK IN ENGLISH SUMMARY **90**

GLOSSARY **94**

ABOUT THE AUTHOR **96**

DEDICATION **98**

BIBLIOGRAPHY **99**

WHY I WROTE THIS BOOK

I'm not interested in communication,
I'm interested in **accurate worldwide** communication!

And I don't mean among politicians or the elite few. I mean among all of the people, not just the privileged few. I hope that everybody who has something to contribute to humanity and our mistreated planet will have a voice that can be understood by anyone.

English is the bridge language for communication (Lingua Franca). It leads the way professionally, academically and socially because of its dominant role in business, technology, science and entertainment. In order to contribute to any of these fields, it is necessary to have one common language that everyone can understand. That common language is English, but...

Students regularly lose scholarships, promotions or careers because of low English scores

It is heartbreaking to see so many students around the world who have been through years of studying English and are still unable to communicate in the language. What can we do to achieve a better success rate and improve motivation to learn the language? What specific tools and content do we need to prevent these failures from happening?

It is also heartbreaking that well-intentioned ESL/EFL teachers are saddled with administrative obligations and not provided with enough opportunities for professional development often enough. They lack the necessary time to search for motivational materials or do appropriate research. They often don't have the necessary tools and content for the specific needs of their individual students. Their classes are frequently too large for optimal language acquisition.

Yet they are blamed when their students cannot compete or they cannot function in the global community after graduation.

My aim is to help ESL/EFL teachers make English easier for all learners by prioritizing what is needed in their ESL/EFL program. In this book, I want to start with the first step: *How to Think in English*. This provides a solid base for beginners and something to be revisited regularly by advanced students.

An unexpected event came to me like a flash of lightning!

In the blink of an eye and the form of a very advanced student I realized what to prioritize and how to take that first step. I aim to share this with you and help you prioritize your strategies and put your best foot forward.

This book is not meant to be a formal grammar book. It only covers what I consider the first building block of English and offers lots of examples, metaphors and humor, for the sake of clarity. If teachers have a clear aim, they can make acquisition simple and fun for learners.

Thinking in English is the 'potting soil' in which we plant the English tree. It provides speakers of other languages a start in understanding how the English language functions. And it can even be an eye-opener for advanced students who are reviewing basics!

Let's get grounded and teach our students to "Think in English"!

HOW CAN THIS BOOK HELP YOU?

When I first began teaching English to speakers of other languages I longed for a book or some form of guidance that would help me give them a good start. Among the books I had available, I didn't find one that gave me clarity about how the language functioned at its core and that offered the most indispensable tools needed for a solid foundation.

What must I prioritize so my students can get a solid grasp of what they are learning?

After years of trial and error, I isolated what I felt were the four essential building blocks of the language and categorized them in order of difficulty, from concrete to abstract. It covered what I considered to be the basics, until something more fundamental appeared in the form of a student who came for help at the Writing Center where I was working. She was an English major about to graduate and become an English teacher. It was not until this moment that the concept slapped me across the face giving me an additional core building block. It was one that I had known about but had never considered.

Up to that point, I only had a handle on the tools needed by English learners to lead them from concrete to abstract, but I had ignored the bedrock of the language. The student gifted me something that was even more fundamental: the ground for all the tools I had found so far.

In order to use the vital English tools effectively, you first had to Think in English!

ENDORSEMENTS

"Leona Wellington can be considered one of the best ESL/EFL teachers we have ever had at University of Nizwa. She has made a clear difference through her competence in the field, professionalism, and impressive personality. She still stands out with her relentless effort to improve our teaching practices, and to be a role model for other teachers."

~Ayatollah Labadi, Professor of Applied Linguistics, Advisor to the Chancellor for The Foundation Program and Open-Learning, University of Nizwa, Sultanate of Oman~

"I found Leona's book to be full of new information and her method of explaining the structures, rules and roots of the English language are essential for every English learner. I hope people from all over the world will obtain her book because of its high quality."

~Yusuf Alimukhammad, Translator, Commentator and Independent Talk Host~

"Having studied Leona's book with its revolutionary approach, I am convinced that her base principles of English can easily be acquired while bypassing much of the tedious grammar presented in other methods. She makes her students' lives so much easier, and learning so much fun! Thank you, Leona, for presenting this wonderful work to ESL/EFL teachers and students around the world."

~Dr. Syed Rizwan PhD/Communication Trainer, Lucknow, India~

"As an educational professional, Leona is an advocate of providing a holistic approach to learning English for second language learners through dynamic and engaging personalized learning activities conducive to overall language acquisition."

~Derek O'Connell, Director of the Writing Center University of Nizwa, Oman~

"Leona actively utilizes left and right brain modalities to learn and teach. Having a strong background in teaching different subjects in various countries, she is also a professional actor and puppeteer. As charismatic as she is passionate and thorough, any student or fellow learner who has the good fortune to meet Leona will never forget the experience."

~Milton B. Knutson, author and PhD, in French and Spanish Literature, University of Arizona~

"Leona's enthusiasm, energy and good will demonstrates on the intellectual as well as the professional level how to deal with and surmount the challenges and unexpected situations that arise within the context of a public education system. Her humanity as well as her congeniality allows her to make the best of whatever social milieu she finds herself in. As a teacher, Leona needs no recommendation since anyone who meets her immediately recognizes both her personal and professional abilities."

~Don Emilio Arias Martinez, High School Principal, Liceo La Virgen, Costa Rica~

"Leona is a very interactive teacher who motivates students to study and search on their own. She also gives them lots of activities to improve their language skills. In addition, she's able to understand each student's way of learning and aligns herself to their way in order to help them reach their learning goals."

~Humaid Al Salmi, member of the Lifelong Learning staff, University of Nizwa~

"It was such an opportunity to be one of your students. You are one of the best teachers because you make English easier to understand. You also have a unique way of communicating to your students of different ages. I would like you to be my teacher again if possible!"

~Thabit Said Saayid Al-Fazari, Accountant-Finance UNizwa/Member of Leona's Communications Course for Lifelong Learning Institute~

It's rare to come across such a talented teacher like Leona Wellington. I had the pleasure of meeting her at the Writing Center where she helped and guided me to finish the thesis for my M.Ed. (TESOL) I was particularly impressed by her ability to help me edit effortlessly as well as improve my self-esteem and work hard and honestly to be successful.

~Malek Nasser Al Qanoobi, English teacher at Al-muthanna bin Haritha School in Oman~

Leona is not only gifted in ESL/EFL but in other spheres such as linguistics, art and psychology. She has a magnanimous personality and turns the teaching learning process into a magical enjoyable experience with excellent results.

~Olga Chernyshova, English lecturer in Foreign language department, University of Nizwa, Oman~

INTRODUCTION

THE 'AHA' MOMENT

I'd known the fact for a long time
But it wasn't until that moment
That I acquired the knowledge

The idea struck me like lightning one day when a student walked into the Writing Center where I was working. She came to seek help with her final year project. I want to make it clear that I love helping English Majors and teachers! I know that if I can help them, they will be able to help countless students in the future.

She was about to graduate from university and embark on a career teaching English as a foreign language (EFL). I asked her to show me the manuscript of her final year project but when she did, I was thunder struck!

I could not understand a thing she was trying to say!

As I tried to make sense out of her paper, I realized three things:

1. She had most likely used a translation app.
2. She was not *'Thinking in English'* (SVO-Subject/Vert/Object) when forming her sentences.
3. After years of study, she had missed the main modus operandi of the language.

Her vocabulary was excellent but when she attempted to put her thoughts down on paper she was thinking in her native language.

Of course, this happens all the time, especially under stress, when students are at very advanced levels. But it just made me realize that every ESL/EFL learner needs to start from the ground up and remain grounded as they spiral upward in their learning!

THE THREE SLOTS

I told her that she would need to re-write her paper completely. She gave me a blank stare and before I could stop myself I blurted out the following:

LOOK, JUST DO THIS:

ONE, TWO, THREE

For every sentence you create, ask yourself the following questions:

1. *Who* or *What* am I talking about? -- SLOT NUMBER <u>ONE</u>.
2. *What* is *Who* or *What <u>doing</u>,* (or <u>*being*</u>)? -- SLOT NUMBER <u>TWO</u>.
3. *Who* or *What,* if anybody, is receiving the action -- SLOT NUMBER <u>THREE</u>.

It is as simple as that:

ONE, TWO, THREE

I told her that if she did this she would be pretty correct. I assured her that this was the correct order and each of the three components strictly followed that order. Furthermore, if number THREE had nothing to receive, that was ok.

> *It was only indispensable for it to be in the third position when it had to be a receiver.*

Then I instructed her to look for additional information that answered questions like, HOW, WHEN, WHERE, or WHY the action was happening.

This information could be included after the third slot,
at the end of the sentence.

What I didn't tell her, and I'll say this in a whisper in case beginning students are eavesdropping, is that additional information is often put at the beginning, since it is NOT the core of the sentence. It's only additional information. But the core and kernel of the sentence has to follow SVO order:

ONE, TWO, THREE

The ONE TWO THREE pattern makes it easier for students in the foundation stage to get used to the rhythm and order of SVO so I personally prefer adding additional information in, or after the last slot, as a matter of habit during the foundation stage. My advice is:

Place both object (direct and indirect) and any
additional information at the end.

Once students have acquired the basic word order for thinking in English, they can play with additional information so long as they do not tamper with the SVO core sentence.

Two Examples:

1. The *animals* *ate* their *food* every day at the reserve.
'SVO 'is italicized and underlined as the core sentence.
"every day at the reserve" (additional information about when/where is placed at the end).

2. Every day at the reserve the *animals* *ate* their *food*.
'SVO' is italicized and underlined as the core sentence.

"Every day at the reserve," (additional information about when/where is placed at the <u>beginning</u>).

Students need to maintain their FOCUS on the core sentence. All else is secondary. It will be easy enough to change the position of the additional information later on. The core building block is in SVO, and that is what this book is about.

ONE, TWO, THREE

DID IT SINK IN?

The student left with the task of re-doing her manuscript with SVO in mind. I was doubtful. I kept whispering to myself: "*...about to graduate...will be teaching EFL...hasn't learned this yet...*" But I was shocked a couple of weeks later when she returned with her re-written document. I looked at the manuscript and was now able to understand it.

> *Realizing that SVO is the potting soil for the English tree was my 'aha' moment.*

I'd *known* for a long time that SVO was very important but it was not until my experience with that student that I *acquired* the knowledge. It dawned on me that working and building with SVO can even help advanced students who may already be fossilized (Han Z. 2004).

Helping beginners is crucial, and helping advanced students who are way past foundation and entrenched in poor language habits is also a great concern among ESL/EFL teachers worldwide. I suddenly felt reassured that there might be some help even for advanced students to get back on track. I hoped it was not too late for them.

After all, fossilization is the major problem facing second language teachers worldwide.

SVO CAN SHOCK ADVANCED STUDENTS

I felt that if this one core SVO building block can enable a student to go from incomprehensible to comprehensible, why can't it help other advanced students whose English is a little wobbly?

It might not be able to 'center' them completely, but it is a coping mechanism for students who have to work with material which is over their heads (usually written material).

I later tested SVO on other students who came for help. Of course, they had heard of it but were shocked to re-visit its importance for expressing thoughts in English. In fact, they were angry that they had not realized that SVO is the portal to thinking in English and voiced their opinion about it.

"I'm very grateful to Ms. Leona who taught me from her heart without being boring, and helped me 'think in English'. I thank her for all her help with my final year project."

Hanan Sulaiyam Said Al Shekaili

CHAPTER I

THE THREE BROTHERS LAW

HOW TO THINK IN ENGLISH

I have personified SVO as the Three Brothers Law. This idea came to me in the Middle East where family bonds are so close. SVO is like a closely-knit family unit consisting of three brothers. Think of them as Siamese triplets, bound side by side.

The brothers must stand in a specific order. They are so closely bonded that they always hold hands so nothing can come between them. They remain together in that order without changing places. I find that it is easier for students to think in English if they visualize these three brothers holding hands and assuming their correct positions.

The first brother takes the place of the **Subject**, the second, the **Verb**, and the third, the **Object**.

I will describe the brothers one by one as if they were real people. This visual concept adds a little humor, especially because the third brother has more flexibility than the first two and often turns out to be quite a mischievous little rascal, much to the annoyance of English learners.

WHAT IS SVO?

Subject/Verb/Object (SVO) is the bedrock of English which can be summed up in one word: ORDER. In English, everything has a place and everything has to be put in its place, especially Subject Verb Object word order.

1. ORDER is the thing that makes the language efficient and to the point.
2. ORDER is the thing that keeps the language COMPREHENSIBLE!
3. ORDER is the thing that decides the function of words

SLOT 1 (NOUN PHRASE)

We'll start with slot number one, the first and oldest brother aka—subject of a sentence or clause.

The SUBJECT is always equal to a noun or noun phrase

EIGHT ASPECTS OF 'S' IN SVO:

1. Sentences or dependent clauses start with a noun (phrase).
2. Noun phrases can be a proper noun, a pronoun or even a very long noun phrase.
3. Noun phrases themselves also follow a certain ORDER.
4. Nouns phrases with a singular noun start with a *determiner* to determine their '*nounship*'.
5. Plural or non-countable noun phrases may not need a *determiner* if they are universal.
6. Proper nouns or subject pronouns don't need a *determiner* but may have appositives (optional).
7. Subject nouns and phrases can be pronominalized (represented) by (I/you/he/she/it/we/they).
8. Subjects can be preceded with extra information (how/when/where/why).

A NOUN IS A NOUN IS A NOUN

Let's give nouns some thought. The first way to describe them is that nouns are a person, a place, or a thing. This is a pretty accurate description but there is one problem.

In English, it is sometimes impossible to know for sure if a word is a noun!

A word that names a person, place or thing should be a noun, but in English it may travel incognito as another part of speech! So how can we trust it? What we call a noun might end up morphing out of recognition and become a verb or an adjective.

A noun is not a noun because of its meaning but because of its function and its function is determined by where it is placed in a sentence or phrase. For this reason, nouns can be pretty squirrelly. That is why we need determiners to grab them and keep them in their place! The function of a determiner is just that: to determine that the noun is indeed a noun.

With almost no conjugations in English, it is hard knowing who is doing what to whom!

S

IN SVO

THE FIRST BROTHER:

Slot number one, the S in SVO: the first and oldest brother starts the sentence or clause. This brother's duty is to be the noun (or noun-phrase) that initiates, acts or is something or someone that leads the action of the sentence. As the first and oldest brother that is his responsibility.

He must be able to prove he is a S noun, through pronominalization (the ability to be replaced by a subject pronoun). No matter how long the subject is, it can always be pronominalized or substituted with, I/you/he/she/it/we/they. As the oldest brother, S is the provider, author, sender, or responsible party, for that sentence or clause.

We will have lots of fun building monster noun phrases in this book. But for now, let's just say that the core elements of a sentence start with a noun phrase which is the first to go 'on stage'.

A noun phrase is always going to be a noun phrase even when it is dressed as a pronoun or is simply a proper noun such as 'George McGee or John Doe'. And it will still be a noun even if it is the object of a sentence.

Yes! Noun phrases can also be the object of a sentence. The important thing is their placement. Are they in first position? For that we have to consider what side of the fence they are on. If it is *before* the verb, it will be the subject of that sentence or clause.

Make an evaluation. Is the noun phrase before, or after, the verb?

As far as the bedrock of our foundation program SVO is the most important consideration. Sometimes sentences do not have objects but they must always have a subject. And that subject is a noun which comes before the verb.

SENTENCES DRESS DIFFERENTLY

Why is SVO the bedrock of English? How does SVO make English efficient, blunt and to the point? Why do some sentences not have an object? If we throw the language up in the air, why must it land in its correct position, like a cat, to remain comprehensible?

There is one reason why order is so important. The nature of ENGLISH VERBS themselves is the hidden culprit. Verbs function quite differently in English than in many other languages. They don't have a lot of morphing power and simply need to be 'carried' on stage by the subject. It is the job of the oldest brother (S) to do this in order to get the show going.

English verbs hardly function at all except for their innate meaning (action they represent).

THE LAZIEST PRIMA DONNAS EVER

I see English verbs as the most elite and lazy members of the language. They sit around in hammocks, drinking lemonade and waiting for the first brother (S) to pick them up and carry them on stage so they can deliver their song of action or state of being.

Verbs give you almost zero information about who is doing the action. In fact, they only give you one tiny tip, a sudden burst of sound—that infamous little 's' at the end of the verb for 3rd person singular. When we see that little 's' the author of the action has to be: *he, she,* or *it.*

Unfortunately, it is such a small clue that most learners of English as a second or foreign language don't bother to learn it at all! Instead they may carry this error for years on end and say things like:

"She drive_ fast"

Were it not for that little 's' at the end of the verb, English would probably be a piece of cake. As shown in the example above, learners often don't bother. After all, in their language verbs may be skillful contortionists that can morph to carry their subjects within themselves, instead of expecting subjects to carry them.

This lazy characteristic of English verbs makes it necessary to start sentences or clauses with a noun or subject. There is no way around it as far as I know.

The purpose of this book is to cover the three SVO components so you can help your students think in English with a focus on ORDER.

I will mostly cover noun phrases since both S and O fall in that category. Verbs are an extensive topic that comprises the other four building blocks of the language. They will be covered in my next book.

In this book, *How to Think in English*, I will simply establish the *position* of the V on the bedrock of the language. For now, you can visualize the V in SVO as the hub and indispensable part of any sentence or phrase. But despite being such a star, verbs still depend on nouns or subjects to introduce them.

For that reason, when we cover V, the second component in SVO, any verb will do. You might start with simple present or past and work your way up according to the level of your students. This will become obvious within the following pages. For now, it is only important to know that:

Without the SUBJECT to lead the VERB, we cannot have a sentence.

MAJOR TYPES OF SENTENCES

Let's examine the most traditional sentences as follows:

USING A TRANSITIVE VERB

S	V	O
Slot 1	Slot 2	Slot 3
Noun Phrase as SUBJECT	**Verb Phrase**	**Noun Phrase as OBJECT**

"I sell apples."

This type of sentence exemplifies SVO because it has a transitive verb (a verb that calls for an object). Other transitive verbs can be: hit, buy, eat, sell, take, import, export.

If I hit, I must hit someone or something. If I eat, buy or sell, I must eat, buy or sell something.

Transitive verbs usually require an object and they are the perfect prototype for SVO. The thing that I sell, is the object of the action of the transitive verb, 'sell'. As such it is also a noun phrase. Transitive verbs give us traditional SVO sentences which follows the 1, 2, 3 order perfectly. See more examples of <u>transitive verbs and a printout chart</u> (URL in Bibliography).

NOTE: Some other languages also have SVO word order but they are often much more flexible than English. They establish the author within the verb form itself so the subject becomes optional.

USING LINKING AND INTRANSITIVE VERBS

S	V	C
Slot 1	Slot 2	Complement
Noun Phrase as SUBJECT	Verb Phrase	Adjective and/or how, when, where, why

Linking verbs don't act upon objects; they link to something else and can take complements

LINKING VERBS:

Linking verbs don't act upon objects; they link to something else and can take complements

1. Sandra *looks* beautiful when she is smiling.

<u>looks</u> links to the adjective: *beautiful (Adj.)*
when she is smiling completes the sentence by explaining *when* she looks beautiful (C)

2. James *is* in the garage.

<u>is</u> links to the prepositional phrase *in the garage* explaining *where* he is (C)

3. Jennifer *is* a dentist.

<u>is</u> links to the noun phrase *a dentist* explaining *what* her profession is (C)

NOTE:

Dentist is not acted upon by Jennifer, it simply equals Jennifer. The linking verb BE is like a balance scale: Jennifer = Dentist. Some other linking verbs are: appear, become, look, act. They can link to an adjective compliment, a noun or another compliment as shown in the examples above. See <u>additional explanations</u> of linking verbs and a quiz to score your understanding (URL in Bibliography).

INTRANSATIVE VERBS:

Intransitive verbs do no take objects but they can take one or more complements

1. They *work* all night at the factory.

all night completes the sentence by explaining *when* they work (C)
at the factory completes the sentence by explaining *where* they work (C)

2. He *smiles* brightly because he knows he won the game.

brightly completes the sentence by explaining *how* he smiles (C)
because he knows he won the game completes the sentence by explaining *why* (C)

3. The five students *go* to the same school because it is close.

the same school completes the sentence by explaining *where* they go (C)
because it is close by completes the sentence by explaining why (C)

Access a quick guide to <u>intransitive verbs</u> and a printable chart (URL in Bibliography). Note how beautifully the examples show extra information placed at the beginning and also explain how *intransitive* verbs can also be *transitive*. Again, this shows how the secret is not in the word itself but its function, according to its placement and how it is used in the sentence.

SV ALONE OR WITH COMPLIMENT

S	**V**
Slot 1	Slot 2
Noun Phrase	**Verb Phrase:**

The subject and verb are the two indispensable components of a sentence.

The subject is there so we know who the author is. The verb is there so we know what action that author takes. If it is not a transitive verb, that is enough to have a complete sentence.

1. People *dream.*
2. Animals *survive.*
3. Flowers *bloom.*

Any sentence can have a completion telling how
when where or why it happened

1. People *dream* when they go to sleep.
when they go to sleep completes the sentence by explaining *when* they dream (C)

2. Animals *survive* by sheer instinct.
by sheer instinct completes the sentence by explaining *how* they survive (C)

3. Flowers bloom in the desert valley after it rains.
in the desert valley completes the sentence by explaining *where* they bloom (C)
after it rains completes the sentence by explaining *when* flowers bloom

SUBJECT PRONOUNS

THE SEVEN DIPLOMATS

(I / You / He / She / It / We / They)

SINGULAR: ONE DIPLOMAT or REPRESENTATIVE

1. 'I' first person *singular* or the one-person talking
2. '**You**' second person *singular* or the one person spoken to (one you)
3. '**He/She/It**' third person *singular* or the one person spoken about

PLURAL: MORE THAN ONE DIPLOMAT or REPRESENTATIVE

1. '**We**' first person plural or more than one person talking (I+other/s)
2. '**You**' second person plural or more than one person spoken to (**NOTE**: You is both singular and plural but always conjugates like a plural).
3. '**They**' third person plural or more than one person (or thing) spoken about

The function of pronouns is to *represent* nouns. If they are subject pronouns, then their function is to represent the subject. Because subjects are one of the three components of SVO, acquiring the pronouns that represent them is vital for the basic foundation needed to get a good start in the language.

Once the subject is determined, no matter how long it is, the role of a corresponding subject pronoun will be to represent it. It will come before the verb phrase and the verb phrase must agree with it.

Subject verb agreement is where we hear lots of complaints from ESL/EFL teachers. But after pronominalization (substituting the subject with its corresponding subject pronoun) it is easy to make these two match.

Pronouns represent any and all nouns and noun phrases in English.

That **man** = **HE**

That **man** with the striped hat [*that is*] playing the guitar and sitting on the corner = **HE**

Subjects and subject pronouns work hard for their keep. Without them we would not know who is doing what. Remember how hard they have to work to carry all those lazy verbs around so listeners know who the actor is. The verbs are just not going to tell us!

BUT IS IT A SUBJECT OR OBJECT?

BEFORE THE VERB	VERB	AFTER THE VERB
I	VERB	ME
YOU	VERB	YOU
HE	VERB	HIM
SHE	VERB	HER
IT	VERB	IT
WE	VERB	US
THEY	VERB	THEM

Do your students know what side of the fence they are on?

I have met many fourth-year ESL/EFL academic students who don't know what side of the fence they are on (before or after the verb). Make sure your students are not among them. Since we are discussing SVO and since our verbs are so helpless you must insure that your students acquire this concept during the early part of their basic foundation program. The question to remember is: are the pronouns the *givers* or the *receivers*?

MULTITASKING OUTSIDE OF SVO

THE GREAT IMPOSTOR PRONOUNS

DETERMINERS:
ALSO KNOWN AS POSSESSIVE ADJECTIVES OR POSSESSIVE **PRONOUNS**
MY
YOUR
HIS
HER
ITS
OUR
THEIR

These innocent little guys should not be thought of as pronouns at all!

PRONOUNS AS EXTRA FROSTING

REFLEXIVE	POSSESIVE
MYSELF	MINE
YOURSELF	YOURS
HIMSELF	HIS
HERSELF	HERS
ITSELF	ITS
OURSELVES	OURS
THEMSELVES	THEIRS

Do your students use impostors and extra frosting correctly?

PRONOUNS AS GREAT IMPOSTORS

Although the pronouns listed as 'IMPOSTORS' look like normal pronouns, their vital function is really to determine a noun to follow. That is why they should be called determiners and not possessive adjectives or possessive pronouns.

They don't have a side of the fence they must be on for SVO. Nevertheless, *The Big Pronoun Giveaway* activity (following chapter) is a perfect place to use them as it is about giving and receiving objects. And we know that objects (nouns) must be determined so these determiners (otherwise known as possessive adjectives or possessive pronouns) are essentially there to determine a noun. The good thing about using them for the activity is that they link to the subject or indirect object pronouns, indirectly reinforcing SVO.

For beginners, you may also use common determiners like articles 'this/that/the' etc.

PRONOUNS AS EXTRA FROSTING

The pronouns listed as 'EXTRA FROSTING' in the charts are also important and great for practice although they are also somewhat outside the scope of SVO as they are not directly linked to its ORDER. I have included them in the *'The Big Pronoun Giveaway'* Activity because they are excellent for engaging the right brain and are an integral part of English.

Additionally, including these two extra options in the activity is a way of multi-tasking important concepts that are also an important part of English.

So, let's multitask while practicing SVO and having fun with the right brain

NOTE:

The explanations given so far are only meant as a reference for teachers to make sure the principles are clear. They are not meant for memorization or to confuse students. The following, *Big Pronoun Giveaway Activity* will take care of the acquisition of these principles. Acquisition is all that students need and this mostly comes through practice, not the memorization of rules.

ACTIVITY

THE BIG PRONOUN GIVEAWAY:

This is an activity that should be done with beginners to insure acquisition of core language tools. It should also be practiced with higher levels, for reinforcement. It is a fun and easy activity to do at the beginning of basic English studies when students are just learning elementary vocabulary.

For this activity, they can use their own personal objects or objects you provide. Make sure they all have an object to 'give away'. Have students sit in a circle. If it's a small class (3-10) you will only have one group. If it's a larger class, you may need to separate them into smaller groups. If you have several groups, try to get a helper to monitor and make sure the group uses the correct subject and object pronouns.

1. One student starts by giving and saying directly to another student, "I give YOU my _____.

2. That same 'giver' then turns and tells the rest of the group: "I give HIM/HER my _____.

3. The student that receives the object says to the giver: "YOU give ME your _____.

4. The same 'receiver' says to the rest of the group: "HE/SHE giveS me his/her _____.

5. The next student repeats what has been given so far and adds their own object in the same manner.

6. Each subsequent student repeats what has already been given by the other students and adds their own until all the students have given, received and told the receiver and the group what has been given and received.

7. Of course, the last student gets the wonderful task of repeating all that has taken place.

8. At the end, the more daring students can volunteer to describe all the giving and receiving that took place for the whole group

NOTE:

The transitive verb 'give' is a perfect verb to use for this practice. If students are more advanced this is not only an excellent subject and object pronoun review for them, it can include present, past, or future tenses (more multitasking):

I *will give* (before the fact); I *give* (as you are giving) and 'I *gave*' after the fact. Use these simple verb tenses unless your students can manage other more advanced verb tenses such as 'I have given'. Choose the verb tenses at your discretion. The essential practice is about subject and object pronouns in relation to SVO, not about verb tenses.

Practicing with 'possessive pronouns' as determiners and different verb tenses is an excellent way of multitasking while affirming SVO. We will cover more about this in the activity: *'Build the Wildest Subject.'*

EXTENSION ONE—SOME FROSTING

If your students are more advanced, you could practice with the reflexive pronouns from the chart (PRONOUNS AS EXTRA FROSTING). This is a way of engaging the right brain by adding emphasis to the practice. Like a mirror reflexive pronouns are meant to make the action reflect back on the subject or giver. It sounds a little better to use the past tense for this practice to add a little more 'astonishment.'

I—myself
You—yourself
He—himself
She—herself-
It—itself
We—ourselves
They—themselves

She gave her_____ to them, *herself.*
They gave their_____ to us, *themselves.*
We gave our_____ to them, *ourselves.*

Conversely you could say:

I, *myself*, gave my_____ to him.

She, *herself*, gave her_____ to them.

They, *themselves*, gave their _____ to us.

We, *ourselves*, gave our _____ to them.

The last two examples above can be a follow up practice between two groups or pairs of students. Each pair or group gives to the other pair or group. This enables the use of WE and US.

NOTE:

Use these reflexive pronouns orally with strong theatrical emotion as if you were acting. This really engages the right brain and supports acquisition.

Imagine someone telling you: "you didn't give him your BMW, did you?" And your answer being: "Yes! I gave my BMW to him, *myself!*"

Students will quickly master the reflexives and have fun using them with emphasis:

EXTENSION TWO—RETURN TO OWNER

To end the practice, returning the objects to their owners is another very useful exercise. Put all the objects in the center of the circle. Student volunteers can take turns asking the question:

"Whose _____ is this?"

The rest of the students can point to the real owner or themselves and say: "It is *mine / yours / his / hers / ours / theirs*. You probably don't need to use '*its*' unless you have a smart animal or robot in the group!

For optimal use of the right brain, be very emphatic in exposing the owner. You can even stage face to face arguments about ownership of the items.

"It's *MINE!*" or "It **IS** mine!

"No, it's *MINE!*" (*yours/his/hers/ours/theirs*)

Engaging the right brain in this manner really supports acquisition and peppers motivation.

This kind of practice can be done periodically with new vocabulary to reinforce the subject and object pronouns as well as the extra 'frosting'. It practices what side of the fence they are on in SVO, our bedrock building block, and it facilitates language acquisition as opposed to learning or memorizing rules.

NOTE:

1. When each person finally gets their object back they can say: This _____ is MINE.
2. Make sure to choose interesting objects with names that are not too difficult or long. They only need to be difficult enough to suit the level

of the learners. The key is for the objects to be interesting enough to captivate their imagination, not to create stumbling blocks during the activity or bore the students to tears. Avoid objects such as pencil, eraser or notebook if possible. These objects will be learned anyway, and are not interesting or challenging.

3.   The names for the objects also provide additional vocabulary (which will have been acquired by the end of the practice) not to mention that interesting vocabulary also engages the right brain which motivates and scaffolds acquisition.

4.   This practice 'sets up' an SVO situation by having students (S) give items to others in the group who are the receivers (O).

5.   Our focus is not on the direct (O) (object that is given) but on the person who receives the item (indirect O).

6.   The item itself that is given (direct object) is covered below in "OBJECTS HAVE TWO FACES".

7.   The key here is that the giver is in the first slot and the receiver is in the third. The long term aim for this activity is to practice the pronouns that correspond to givers and receivers. Students need to acquire the automatic usage of the correct subject pronouns (I/you/he/she/we/they) as well as the correct object pronouns (me/you/him/her/it/us/them).

Because of their position within SVO, subject and object pronouns are vital acquisition points for students and the key is always what side of the verb the noun phrases are on and how these noun phrases are represented by their corresponding pronouns.

EXAMPLE:

The first graders loved the teacher.

(S) the <u>first graders</u> = THEY
(V) loved

(O) the <u>teacher</u> = HER

They loved *her*

The teacher loved the first graders.

(S) <u>the teacher</u> = SHE
(V) loved
(O) the <u>first graders</u> = THEM.

She loved *them*

ADDITIONAL ACTIVITY CONSIDERATIONS

OBJECTS HAVE TWO FACES

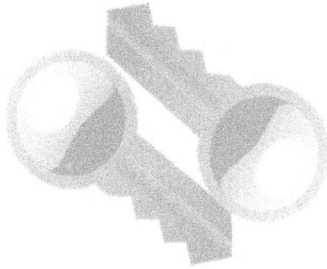

Transitive verbs can have two types of objects: *direct* and *indirect*. They almost always must have a *direct* object but don't necessarily need *indirect* object. As objects, both direct and indirect must come after the verb. You can think of them as extensions or results of the verb phrase.

The thing I buy (sell/throw/kick/ride) is the direct object (D.O.) and the person I buy it for, is the indirect object, (I.O): The indirect object receives the direct object (sent by the first brother). It is usually better to list the direct object first.

I deliver the newspaper to Susan.

(S) = I
(V) = deliver
(O) = the newspaper = IT
(I.O) = to Susan = HER

If the D.O. or the I.O. are already known, you can use the direct and indirect object pronouns to replace either or both.

I deliver *it* to *her.*

For the activity, *The Big Pronoun Giveaway*, our aim is to practice the indirect object pronouns because there are more of them: *me/you/him/her/us/them*. Direct objects are usually 'things' that the subject acts upon which equates to '*it*' and '*them*' (one, or more than one, 'thing' acted upon).

Of course, it is possible that I might kick a person, such as, George. In this case my foot directly affects George, so HIM which might be an indirect object, becomes the direct object.

I kick HIM.

Of course, we usually kick a ball, or the wall, rather than a person.

More examples:

I bought a trampoline.

(S) = I
(V) = bought
(D.O.) = a <u>trampoline</u> = IT

I bought a trampoline for the children.

(S) = I
(V) = bought
(O) = a trampoline = IT
(I.O) = for the children = THEM
I bought *it* for the children.
I bought *it* for *them*.

Although both direct and indirect objects come after the verb, they don't always have the same order. One is usually described and the other takes the object pronoun.

I sent flowers to Jennifer.

I sent flowers to <u>her</u>.

I sent <u>her</u> flowers

If the direct object or the indirect object vary, just use the corresponding object pronoun. Clarity of meaning is what is important. Sometimes it is better to write out the word rather than to use pronouns that are confusing.

I bought the cookies for the neighbors.

I bought *them* for the neighbors.

I bought the cookies for *them*.

I bought *them* the cookies.

NOTE:

Two object pronouns can be used if the listener knows what the D.O. and I.D. are. Plural direct

and indirect object pronouns use the same word THEM, so you simply have to use common sense.

I bought *them* for *them*.

Since the acquisition focus on *The Big Pronoun Giveaway* activity is subject pronouns (S) and Indirect object pronouns (I.O.), you don't need to say the names of the 'giver' and 'receiver' during the activity. Instead, you can point your finger at the corresponding person, pair or group.

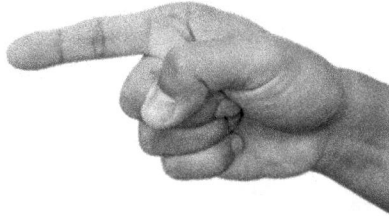

***Pointing may not be socially polite, but it gets the
job done for this activity!***

Remember, if it were not for subject and object nouns, and pronouns, and where they are placed in relation to the verb, we really wouldn't know who gives and who receives. They are both part of thinking in English.

Our students simply need to know what side of the fence (V) they are working with. And they need to know it quickly and automatically without having to think or figure it out. Language acquisition is a skill like any other skill—it requires *practice*, (lots of *practice)*, to master.

V

IN SVO

CHAPTER II

SLOT 2 (VERB PHRASE)

BUT THERE ARE THOUSANDS OF VERBS!

There are regular, irregular, transitive, intransitive, linking, complicated phrasal verbs, with myriads of idiomatic meanings etc. Yes, English has lots of verbs. In fact, nobody seems to know how many, according to my research. And don't forget how lazy these Prima Donnas are!

All I can say is that it keeps English pronouns
off of unemployment compensation!

THE HUB OR STAR OF THE SHOW

The second slot in SVO, belongs to the second brother whose only duty is to carry out the action or state of being for the first brother, regardless of what kind of verb phrase is used.

This book will not cover all the combinations of verbs and verb phrases. Its aim is simply to reserve the second slot for the verb or verb phrase. I suggest using past simple and present simple verbs for beginners and more complex verb phrases, according to the level of your students.

I will cover verbs and verb phrases in detail in my next book. If you are subscribed to receive my weekly updates and tips, you will be notified when the book is out. Verb phrases comprise four of the five building blocks of the language. In fact, I thought there were only these four building blocks until my 'aha' moment.

For thinking in English with SVO, our students just need to know that when the subject or first brother is complete, the verb or verb phrase must follow immediately and it is the second brother's job to do this.

At this point you will realize that the *pronominalization* of the subject to a subject pronoun (I/you/he/she/it/we/they) will make subject verb agreement easy. Fortunately, there are not too many ways to go wrong with subject verb agreement if we have assigned a pronoun to represent the subject.

HOW TO GET ALONG WITH THE STAR

Once a long complicated subject is reduced to a subject pronoun, subject verb agreement becomes easy. There are only two things to remember with present and past simple:

1. *He/she/it* will need to add an 's' after the verb for present simple. This will take practice.
2. All subject pronouns: *I/you/he/she/it/we/they* use the SAME past tense form. This is easy.

PRESENT:

Our boss [he/she/it] / **PLANS** an outing.
[I/you/we/they] **PLAN** an outing.

PAST:

[I/you/he/she/it/we/they] **PLANNED** an outing.

IN CONCLUSION:

Make it simple, just practice whatever verb forms you are covering depending on the level of the students and use the simple ones for beginners like the simple present and simple past just covered.

This is a very brief summary of V in SVO but it is a placeholder for the second brother, the VERB PHRASE.

If you want an in-depth understanding of verb phrases you will find it in my upcoming ESL/EFL book. Sign up to receive updates about the release of the book. I guarantee you will be thrilled and amused to become acquainted with the prima donnas of English covered in the four subsequent building blocks.

SVO is simply the bedrock that underpins the other four building blocks.

Additionally, my book covers the core principles for good teaching practice, as well as first and second language acquisition considerations. It will give you a thorough understanding of all the components needed to teach more effectively and how to make sure that your students get the hands-on practice they need to acquire English in a holistic manner that is fun, easy and makes sense.

You are also welcome to call me for a FREE 15-minute consultation about the particular issues you want to resolve in your own ESL/EFL practice or school. To check out other resources and learn more about our mission, go to: www.leonawellington.com

And if you want a very comprehensive hands-on in depth grasp of the 'Second Brother' or V in SVO, you may also schedule a presentation or workshop for your school or district.

Thinking in English is not about complex verb phrases,
it's about SVO word order

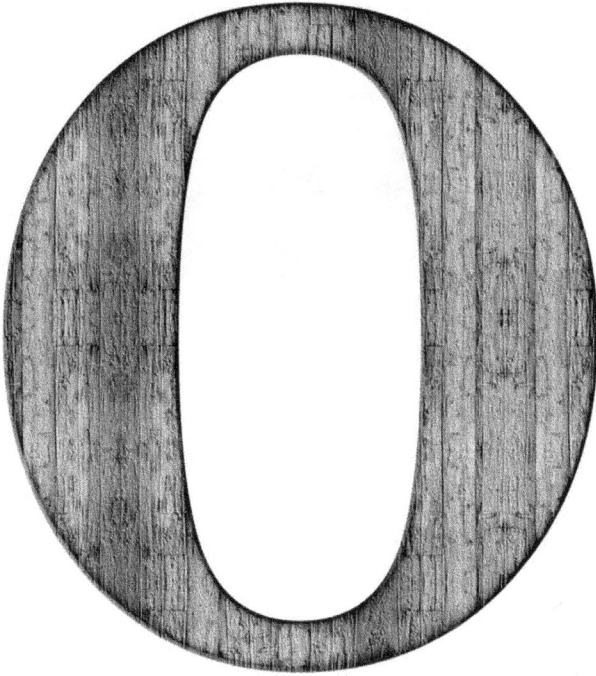

O

IN SVO

CHAPTER III

SLOT 3 (OBJECT/COMPLEMENT)

THERE'S A BLACK SHEEP IN EVERY FAMILY

This slot belongs to the 3rd brother. Being the youngest, he often has no duties! For shame! How spoiled can the youngest sibling be? He has only one very important duty, which he often does not need to carry out. You could say his duties are unpredictable! Nevertheless, his inescapable duty is to fill the 3rd slot, whenever he needs to do so.

This happens if the 1st brother sends something through the action (transitive verb) of the 2nd brother. Then the 3rd brother has to be ready to receive it and he has to be ready to prove he is a capable receiver. To do this, he must be able to pronominalize the O with one of the object pronouns: me/you/him/her/it/us/them.

He cannot avoid this duty unless there is nothing to receive which can happen (intransitive and linking verbs) but he can still add information to complete the sentence. This additional information should fall in the 3rd slot or after it, especially for learners who are just getting used to ORDER through the Three Brothers Law.

The additional information is referred to as a compliment (C) and can be added to any sentence despite the type of sentence or type of verb. It is not the object of a transitive verb.

The third brother is allowed to be a bit mouthy and can add this type of gossipy information to complete or explain what the first two brothers have done, like *how, when, where* or *why* it was done.

These compliments usually come at the end of the 3rd slot, but when this young rascal feels particularly naughty, he can even butt in and add this information before the older brother begins the sentence. The oldest brother is not too happy about this, but there is nothing he can do about it!

The youngest sibling can easily get away with it, because the gossipy information is not part of the core sentence.

> *"I can gossip before you, if I want to!" retorts the young sibling to his older brother.*

The one thing he can never do however, is to come between his two older brothers and if there is something to catch, he has to be in the 3rd slot in order to catch it.

In this manner, the three brothers control the language through ORDER and they always stay side by side, not allowing anything to separate them. Their slots have to be filled by the corresponding brother who has to be in his correct position.

It is as simple as that and in order to make sure the law is upheld the three brothers always hold hands, except when the youngest slips away to have fun and do his shenanigans, if he has nothing to catch, and just because he can.

COMPLIMENTS VERSUS OBJECTS

Transitive verbs require an object (SVO) although a compliment can be a placeholder for the object as shown in the third example below. Sometimes compliments can even precede the subject as shown in the fourth example. Doing this gives the youngest brother rollicking pleasure and allows him luxurious poetic license. If the compliment is missing however, an object must go in the third slot to uphold the *Three Brother's Law*. See the fifth example below:

1. The housewife buys apples (SVO).

(S) The housewife
(V) buys
(O) apples

2. The housewife buys apples at the fair (SVOC)

(S) The housewife
(V) buys
(O) apples
(C) at the fair

We can omit the object and put the compliment in its place by assuming the listener knows what the object is or that the housewife does buy things at a certain place:

3. The housewife buys at the fair (SVC)

(S) The housewife
(V) buys
(C) at the fair

And as long as the Object is still there, it would be acceptable, though not optimal, to say:

4. At the fair, the housewife buys apples (CSVO)

(C) at the fair
(S) the housewife
(V) buys
(O) apples

But it would not be acceptable to omit the object if there is no compliment to cover for it. As you can see, omitting the object when the compliment moves to the beginning, doesn't work:

5. At the fair the housewife buys (CSV) (Buys what?)

(C) at the fair
(S) the housewife
(V) buys

SUMMARY OF EXAMPLES:

Because 'buy' is a transitive verb which needs an O, even if we have to guess what the object is, as in the third example, we are satisfied to accept the C to complete the idea. We assume the reader already must know what it is that the housewife buys or that she shops for different items at the fair.

This is one more good reason to keep compliments (C) at the end, for beginning students. Even though transitive verbs 'require' objects, objects can sometimes be bypassed in SVO but generally SVO remains SVO.

WHY DO WE NEGLECT THE OBVIOUS?

As strange as it may seem, some ESL/EFL teachers don't realize what an orderly language English is. Native speakers just use order correctly because they are native speakers. It doesn't occur to them that learners need to have an awareness of order from the beginning.

After all, in English it is comprehensible to say: 'She bakes bread (SVO) but not, 'Bread she bakes (OSV) or even 'Bakes bread she' (VOS) or 'Bakes she bread' (VSO) or Bread bakes she (OVS). Yet these other orders are the prevalent orders in other world languages (Brinton 2000).

I'm a native speaker so I never gave order much thought. I just assumed that everyone would think the same way I did or order their sentences in the same 'logical' way. I was shocked to find out that less than half the languages in the world have the same word order that we do in English and that the most used word order in the world is SOV (She bread bakes)!

I knew SVO but didn't know that I knew it. So how could I expect my students to know it?

I first consciously learned about word order when I took an Applied Linguists seminar and I was shocked by what our teacher, Dr. Marguerite Mahler (2004) showed us about word order, along with our textbook, *The Structure of Modern English* (Brinton 2000).

Word order is obvious to us when it is our language but we neglect it because it IS so obvious and because it IS our language!

How could something so important as word order have gone over my head during all the time I had been teaching EFL? For shame! I had never given it a second thought! The word order I had been using seemed 'logical' to me.

Word order is also not as important at the beginning when students learn: *"The Boy likes cars"* but it becomes imperative when students read or write long academic subjects.

Based on the three main functions of Subject, Verb and Object, Dr. Mahler pointed out that six logical word orders resulted, worldwide. They are the following, with the percentage of languages that use them:

SOV—46%
SVO—43%
VSO—8%
VOS—2%
OVS—1%

OSV—only one language attested -- in the Amazon basin.

English (SVO) belongs to the second most prevalent category which it shares with many other languages. It is however, still less than 50% of world languages.

As ESL/EFL teachers this is important because other languages, which may be the native languages of our students, either don't share this order with us or can vary it with no repercussions as shown in regard to Spanish, in the following example:

Spanish shares SVO word order with English so the sentence, "The men eat apples." in Spanish is "Los hombres comen manzanas." (exactly the same order as English).

When using pronouns in English, however, we still must use SVO and say: "They eat them." This is because we must use a subject pronoun to identify the 'eater' as our verb doesn't say who 'eats', and 'them' is in last position as the 'object' eaten. Our order still remains the same (SVO).

In Spanish, however we say: "Las comen." (OV). The verb already includes 'they' so we can radically change the order by starting with the object: (them they eat).

It is the impotency of its verbs that makes SVO the rule of rules in English

We must make sure our students incorporate SVO into their English expressions by 'Thinking in English' from the beginning. If not, they may resort to their native language when the going gets tough.

'NAME YOUR SUBJECT'

We can start SVO by pointing to slot number one and asking students to name their subject. Sometimes ESL/EFL students, who have been talking about someone, will start a new sentence with a verb as in: "*goes to super*market."

When this happens, and easy reminder is: '**Who'** goes to the supermarket? It's OK that we may already know who they are referring to, but we still have to make sure the student puts either the subject or its pronoun representative in slot number one.

Verbs in languages like Spanish have more responsibilities and often carry much bigger loads. This gives them more freedom to move around and vary their word order, while still keeping perfect comprehension.

We cannot do this in English because word order is the solid ground from which the language springs; our skeleton; our backbone. Students don't need to *know* this. They just need the general concept and then *acquire* it, through practice, so it comes naturally when they attempt to '*Think in English*'. This is like learning to swim or ride a bike. SVO is the English 'stroke' or 'pedaling technique'. Staying grounded permits English to function correctly and be the first building block of the language.

Additionally, word order even dictates how noun phrases are formed. Since we don't know if a noun will always remain a noun, we start off the noun phrase by using a determiner to nail it down.

NOTE:

The O in SVO, strictly speaking, is also a noun phrase which we have covered along with the subject and object pronouns that represent noun phrases.

Finally, don't forget that the O comes AFTER the verb and has a different set of pronouns to represent it. That being said, I would like to mention a few more things in relation to SVO.

SVO IN RELATION TO CULTURE?

"English is all about 'Time and Money"

Sara Lawrence EFL teacher at Houston Community College in Doha

A staff member, working on his MBA, came to the Writing Center where I was working at the University of Nizwa. He was seeking help with his thesis. His job was to place orders for supplies needed by the university. He commented on the difference between phone conversations with English speakers whose native language is English, as opposed to speakers whose native language is not English.

In both cases English was used as the means of communication.

This student mentioned that those he spoke to, whose native language was English, got right to the point, eliminating small talk that didn't directly relate to the order. Culturally, English means getting straight to the point. SVO gets straight to the point so it is a good start for students from other languages and cultures.

Additionally, a strong value and responsibility is placed on the individual who will carry out the task (the older brother). Starting a sentence with the individual or actor makes it easy to get straight to the point.

For example, the subject pronoun 'I' is so important that it is the only pronoun to be capitalized, regardless of where it is in the sentence. We are taught this in primary school! Yet, why should only 'I' be capitalized?

I

Some people break this rule purposely not wanting to place so much importance on themselves. In the movie, *Seven Years in Tibet*, Brad Pitt was showing off his ice skating moves to the Tibetan seamstress. She commented that she did not understand why Westerners cherished their ego so much, when in her culture people spent their whole lives trying to eliminate the ego.

'I' has a lot of importance for English speakers.

Curiously, I noticed that one student who was writing an autobiographical paper, avoided the 'I' pronoun. I found this very surprising when helping her with her paper because it meant she consistently left out the subject. How could she leave out the subject in an SVO language where the subject is indispensable?

Then I realized it was more than a grammatical omission—
it had to do with her culture.

She admitted feeling very uncomfortable with constantly naming herself in her paper. She disliked starting her sentences with 'I' but could not figure out how to avoid it! And of course, in English she could NOT avoid it, in the kind of paper she was writing, about herself.

Imagine saying:

1. Was born on a Sunday.
2. Attend college in another state.
3. Have two sisters and one brother.

Naturally our question is going to be: "*Who* was born on a Sunday? In her paper, 'I' was missing. The first brother had to come in wearing an 'I' costume to show who *was born*. Of course, the student did not miss the 'I' because in her culture '*was born*' carried its own 'I'.

> *Once SVO is embedded in one's subconscious it becomes easier to* *'Think in English'.*

Finally, it is worth mentioning that academic paragraphs and essays get straight to the point by first announcing the topic, in the topic sentence, before developing the paragraph. It naturally would follow that we start each subsequent sentence by announcing the author (subject) before developing the sentence. That is the nature of SVO and the nature of the culture.

HOW DO I START THE ACTION?

"The journey of a thousand miles begins with one step"
Lao Tzu

Of course, with SVO we start with 'S' aka the subject or noun phrase!

Whatever level your students are in, take a few days at the beginning of the term to play with noun phrases. The simple subject of our sentence will be a noun. The complete subject will be a noun phrase.

If your students are more advanced start the noun phrase with nouns that they don't know and need to learn (like in their area of content—nursing students (injection, capsule, prescription) as opposed to architecture students (design, program, panel).

You may also review basic noun categories. If they know all the common animals, use more unusual or difficult animals like *'poison dart frog'* or *'eyelash viper'*.

YOU 'GOTTA' NAIL DOWN THE NOUN

Textbooks I've seen focus on articles (a/this/that/the etc.) which is well and good, but in fact, students should know that articles are there for a specific reason: to predict a noun. The most important thing about articles is that they are DETERMINERS (determiners of nouns).

Mahler (2005) lists 7 different categories of DETERMINERS: *articles, quantifiers, numerals, demonstratives, possessives, proper noun/possessives, and even words like what and where.* The important thing is not so much how they qualify the noun but that they determine it to be a noun in the first place! So please have your students nail down their nouns!

Develop the noun phrase by determining that
you are introducing a NOUN

ACTIVITY

BUILD THE WILDEST SUBJECT

Have students pick a noun. It is also fun if they choose blindly from a bag full of nouns written on small cards. Or better yet, images of persons, places and things. Next choose a determiner. That is enough to create a SUBJECT. In fact, you may want to stop there for beginners. The show is on! Let the subject noun come on stage. The audience is there waiting to see who the author of the action is. Let's dress and make up our character and give them something to see.

The apple
John's apple
One apple
My apple
This apple
That apple
Any apple
An apple
Our apple
What apple

For the last choice, you can see that 'what' is not a question word but a determiner for apple since apple follows it immediately, instead of a verb. When you continue the sentence, it could become:

What <u>apple</u> we choose, <u>decides</u> the <u>flavor</u> of the pie.

With a determined subject noun in slot number one, you could start a sentence. But don't be in such a hurry! This activity is for developing wild subjects so play with it. Don't worry about what the subjects are going to do yet, just develop their personalities. The first brother should be an interesting character. Dress him up. After all, his job is to bring the prima donna or star onto the stage.

So, have your students create and develop a stockpile of noun phases for the sheer fun of it! There is plenty of time to move onto slot number two later. Developing a subject also means acquiring new vocabulary along the way.

Following are some determiners to choose from to start the S noun phrase. Some are strictly for singular nouns, some for plural nouns and many overlap and can be used for singular or plural nouns. Just make sure students know that the minute you say, 'noun phrase' they need to start with a determiner unless it is a universal plural noun like:

Dogs make great companions.

I don't know about you, but I worry about seeing floating nouns in the ESL/EFL world! So many advanced students totally forget to determine their nouns! They will come up with sentences like:

Chair is in classroom.

Now I might ask: Who is Chair and what or where is 'classroom'? Do you mean 'Cher' is in THE classroom or is classroom a city with a proper name?

Then you wonder if they forgot to capitalize 'classroom,' the name of a city you never heard of before.

So, have your students choose a determiner when they start to build any noun phrase.

Interestingly even nouns in prepositional phrases need to be determined. In fact, when you write a prepositional phrase you start with a preposition and immediately ask yourself, *"what is the object of this preposition."* Then you DETERMINE that object because it is a NOUN.

Example:

On the road (Preposition, Determiner Noun (P/D/N)

(Preposition) on
(Determiner) the
(Object of the preposition) road = *noun*

ABOUT DETERMINERS

Below are some determiners specifically for singular nouns, plural nouns, and both:

FOR SINGLE NOUNS:

A
An
This
That
One

FOR PLURAL NOUNS:

These

Those

Some

Many

Several

Few

Two+

FOR BOTH SINGULAR AND PLURAL NOUNS

The

My

Your

His

Her

Our

Their

My sister's

Dad's

Mary's

etc.

Spend a few minutes to have students choose the determiners they want. They will quickly see how all the determiners require a noun. If I say "*my*" I have to ask, "*my what?*"

I recommend using singular nouns as students must use determiners for them (determiners are not necessarily required for plural nouns). If you use plural nouns match them with plural determiners or neutral determiners. Remember that determiners simply nail down the fact that you are beginning a noun phrase.

SHALL WE BUILD A MONSTER?

Have students build their subject noun phrases and take them as far as they like or can. I'll lead the way in order to create an example. Your students may choose their own variations. Remember we are simply creating different *persons* *places* or *things*' as a SUBJECT (or object) noun phrase. These can begin a sentence (or be the object in a sentence) and can later be replaced by a corresponding subject (or object) pronoun.

1. DETERMINER:

I will choose:

Dad's

Students can supply their own determiner.

NOTE:

Even though the word "*Dad*" itself is a noun, Dad's cannot be the subject because the possessive 's' tells us that the subject is something that belongs to Dad, therefore that 'something' has to be a noun and Dad's becomes the determiner for the upcoming noun.

2. NOUN:

I will choose:

jacket

Students can supply their own noun.

We now have: *Dad's jacket* (D-N)

(D) = Dad's
(N) = jacket

This is as far as it has to go if students are beginners. '*Dad's jacket*' is a complete subject and is able to fill slot number one. But if the level of the students is a little higher we can and should build the subject and take it to monstrous proportions, if possible. This goes according to the students' vocabulary arsenal. To do this, we can add one or more adjectives.

3. ADJECTIVE/S:

An adjective or adjectives come between the determiner and the noun (DAN). What shall we name the monster we are building? He can be: DAN, DAAN or DAAAN! That is up to you.

I will choose the adjective:

leather

Students can supply their own adjective.

We now have: *Dad's leather jacket* (D/A/N)

(D) = Dad's
(A) leather
(N) = jacket

Leather is also a noun but it now becomes an adjective because it comes before jacket. It tells us what kind of jacket belongs to Dad.

This is as far as it has to go. Dad's *leather* jacket is a complete subject and is able to fill slot number one but if students want to add more adjectives and they are able, they can do so. In fact, show them that they can even turn jacket into an adjective, by adding a noun after it!

4. MORE ADJECTIVES?

I will choose:

cleaner

Students can supply their own additional adjectives.

I will place it *after* jacket and now we have: *Dad's leather jacket* cleaner

Why not! This is fun. I chose: cleaner. By adding cleaner at the end, after jacket, cleaner becomes the noun determined by Dad's. That means I'm really talking about the noun: cleaner.

With cleaner as my noun, jacket, which could definitely be considered a noun, becomes an adjective! We now have:

Dad's leather jacket cleaner (D-A-A-N)

(D) = Dad's
(A) = leather
(A) = jacket
(N) = cleaner

NOTE:

Since the noun we really want to determine comes at the end we can often place nouns, adjectives or even verbs before that noun and these will turn into adjectives in function, according to their placement.

5. VERBS:

I will choose:

spray

Students can supply their own verb.

I will place spray before the noun cleaner!

I'm considering 'spray as a verb (although it could be a noun) but by adding spray before the 'noun' cleaner, it becomes an adjective.

We now have: *Dad's leather jacket spray cleaner.* (D-A-A-A-N)

(D) = Dad's

(A) = leather

(A) = jacket

(A) = spray

(N) = cleaner

The determiner: 'Dad's, nails down the nounship and all these words before our established noun, *cleaner,* simply function as adjectives, describing that noun.

Doing this keeps ORDER. Otherwise students might panic about using nouns and verbs as adjectives for *cleaner.*

STOP HERE OR WALK ON THE WILD SIDE

We probably should stop right here as our noun phrase is long enough for a subject but if your students are ready for a wilder ride, you can continue playing with things like *appositives, prepositional phrases* and *clauses.*

Appositives: a word or phrase that describes the subject, is surrounded by commas and could substitute the subject. Using appositives can be a lot of fun but it is optional for beginners.

Prepositional phrases: further describe the subject.

Clauses: add more information related to the last noun mentioned. They can be very tricky because they also have a 'subject' and a verb, but they cannot stand alone, as a sentence. There are many variations but when used after our simple subject they add information about the whole subject, BEFORE getting into the verb phrase (second brother).

Test the waters and surf the waves if your students are able. For beginners, you can keep it simple and add only one, two or none of these.

6. APPOSITIVES (Ap):

I will choose:
<u>a world-famous brand</u>
Students can supply their own appositive.
I will place if after my subject noun with commas around it. Students can do the same.

If we added an appositive to the noun phrase we constructed, it would look like this:

Dad's leather jacket spray cleaner, <u>a world-famous brand</u>, (D-A-A-A-N-Ap)

(D) = Dad's
(A) = leather
(A) = jacket
(A) = spray
(N) = cleaner
(Ap) = a world-famous brand

Either the subject we created, the appositive, or both, could be used as the noun phrase or subject of our sentence, occupying slot number one.

In all of the cases the noun phrase begins with a *determiner*.

1. In the example: Dad's leather jacket cleaner, *cleaner* is our simple subject <u>noun</u>, determined by 'Dad's'.
2. In the example: Dad's leather jacket spray cleaner, a world-famous brand, *a world-famous brand* is the <u>appositive</u>, determined by 'a'.
3. In the example of the complete subject, with the appositive, *cleaner* our simple subject <u>noun</u>, plus a *world-famous brand*, (appositive) is determined by 'Dad's'.

NOTE:

We have come this far so encourage your students to add more and let them play with slot number one, by adding a prepositional phrase that gives additional information about the noun such as where it is located, when it was purchased etc.

7. PREPOSITIONAL PHRASES (P.P):

I will choose:
<u>on the kitchen shelf</u>
Students can supply their own prepositional phrase.

The noun phrase now becomes:

Dad's leather jacket spray cleaner, a world-famous brand, <u>on the kitchen shelf</u>

Finally, they can add clauses, that continue describing the last noun, '*shelf*' telling which '*shelf*'.

8. CLAUSES (Cl):

I will choose:
<u>that Roger built</u>

Students can supply their own clause/s.

We can now add one or more clauses that give additional information about the noun, *shelf,* in our prepositional phrase. After all there could be more than one shelf in the kitchen and we want the listener to look for the cleaner on the correct shelf. Our subject now becomes:

Dad's leather jacket spray cleaner, a world-famous brand, on the kitchen shelf <u>that Roger built.</u>

We started this wild noun phrase with a determiner because we needed to nail down the noun! Carry out this practice only to the level your students can understand. Don't burden beginning students with very long and complicated noun phrases unless they are able to create them and enjoy doing so.

AT LAST!

When the noun phrase is complete, students can pronominalize it! Our simple subject is *cleaner* = IT. We can substitute our whole subject with IT. This is very important because IT (third person singular) allows us to match the verb phrase correctly, like fitting one puzzle piece with another.

THE ACCORDION PRINCIPLE

The practice we just did is like an accordion. We first determine a simple noun. Then we stretch it out as far as our students are capable with the components and the order we just covered. Then we close the accordion and finally it all comes down to the subject pronoun: IT.

Encourage students to make it fun and build on their own simple subject as much as they like.

Here is a summary of how we built the subject noun phrase and can shrink it back down to IT:

Dad's
Dad's jacket
Dad's leather jacket
Dad's leather jacket cleaner
Dad's leather jacket spray cleaner
Dad's leather jacket spray cleaner, a world-famous brand,
Dad's leather jacket spray cleaner, a world-famous brand on the kitchen shelf
Dad's leather jacket spray cleaner, a world-famous brand on the kitchen shelf that Roger built

Dad's leather jacket spray cleaner, a world-famous brand on the kitchen shelf

Dad's leather jacket spray cleaner, a world-famous brand,

Dad's leather jacket spray cleaner

Dad's leather jacket cleaner

Dad's leather jacket

Dad's jacket

Dad's

= IT

The subject pronoun IT, makes it easy to match to the verb which is to follow.

The value of this practice will become apparent when students get to very advanced levels. At that point they will come across many monster subjects that may have any of the elements just covered. If they have already gone through the process of building a long subject, they will be able to comprehend these monsters in advanced readings and writings.

I can also guarantee that when they get to higher academic levels the subjects will NOT be as much fun, so keep the practice light and whimsical. The name of the game is 'fun'.

Once the complete subject S is built we heave a sigh of relief; we know it is represented by the subject pronoun IT and we are ready for the verb.

It is ORDER in the language that makes the language comprehensible so play with ORDER for a few days with the students, regardless of their level. They just need to get the concept of how to build a subject.

They need to know that no matter how ornate or long it is, it will boil down to one subject pronoun. They also need to know that the verb phrase does not start until the subject is finished. If your students are beginners their monster subject can be as simple as:

The black jacket, a Gucci, on the chair that you like = IT

(D) = The
(A) = black
(N) = jacket
(Ap) = a Gucci
(P.P) = on the chair
(Cl) = that you like

= IT

NOTE:

Because our lazy verbs offer so little help, we need SVO to carry us along. Building noun phrases is really enjoyable, especially when you use the right brain to throw in or substitute interesting adjectives. I will suggest ways to use the right brain for the activities below.

1. First have you students build a subject (noun phrase) according to their level (it will be a template).
2. Next you can have them engage their right brain to substitute components of the subject.
3. These subjects can be verbalized in different manners. For right brain reinforcement, have them read the subjects with emotions and rhythms (see chart below).
4. Saying the subject in different ways adds diversity which is fun for the students and supports their verbal and reading skills.
5. Each repetition scaffolds the underlying structures and order you want them to acquire.

EXAMPLES RE-VISITED AND PLAYED WITH:

The black jacket, a Gucci, on the chair that you like = IT

This sentence can become:

The small insect, a golden beetle, in the room that you waxed = IT

(D) = The

(A) = small

(N) = insect

(Ap) = a golden beetle

(P.P) = in the room

(Cl) = that you waxed

= IT

SUBJECTS CAN BE OBJECTS:

(EITHER WAY THEY CAN BE PRONOMINALIZED)

All the examples above can be reversed as shown below since both S and O, in SVO are noun phrases. They can be used in either first or third position. Following is a reversed version of a sample noun phrase. It is followed by its pronominalization (the closed accordion):

Susan threw that black <u>jacket</u>, a Gucci, on the chair that you use.

(S) = Susan

(V) = threw

(D) = that

(A) = black

(N) = jacket

(Ap) = a Gucci

(P.P) = on the chair

(Cl) = that you use

= IT

"She threw IT".

NOTE:

This example shows how the accordion principle simplifies sentences and can turn them into their corresponding pronoun as either subjects or objects. Since 'you' and 'it' are the same as both subject and object you can make the subject plural to practice the different pronouns. For example:

Susan sells some nice <u>perfumes</u>, Armani, in her boutique that's in the mall.

(S) = Susan
(V) = sells
(D) = some
(A) = nice
(N) = perfumes
(Ap) = Armani
(P.P) = in her boutique
(Cl) = that's in the mall

= THEM

"She sells THEM".

ENGAGING THE RIGHT BRAIN

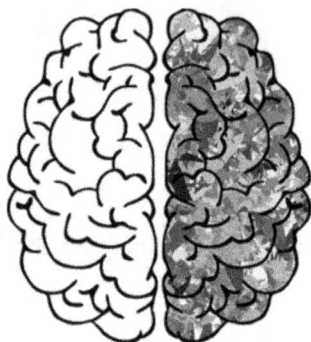

The following chart shows some of the attributes of the right brain which I consider to be indispensable for holistic right brain acquisition.

When SVO is taught to second language learners it is often simply mentioned here and there along the learning process. This has happened to many students I have worked with who knew about SVO but had never given it much thought when they wrote papers and essays.

Students continue learning English and never consciously revisit the concept until it slaps them in the face as they try to write or comprehend their textbooks or difficult academic writing.

This chart suggests emotions or ways of practicing the subjects your students are playing with:

Sound	Volume	Touch	Emotion
Tone	Images	Rhythm	Intention
Sensuality	Pronunciation	Taste	Speed
Smell	Shapes	Humor	

What Would You Do If You Lost Your Left Brain? (chapter in my upcoming book)

LEAN HEAVILY ON THE RIGHT

Have competitions to see how well your students can verbalize the subjects they have created by playing on different moods or attitudes. This can be accomplished through any combination of the attributes shown in the chart above.

After your students have done their subject building activity with the accordion principle, let them use their imagination to show off the subjects they have created. Ways for this are highlighted below. I hope they had fun building an arsenal of subjects! This works for beginners and advanced students both.

STRATEGIES FOR ALL LEVELS

If you are working on Building Block One with advanced students use what you have to work with. For example, use their academic readings or textbooks. These often have monster subjects which we can count on to be correct templates but which many students go crazy trying to decipher. They not only have to figure out the monster sentences but also look up difficult vocabulary.

Students often came to the writing center with their textbooks which they were unable to understand. One-on-one we would go through the academic writing in their books to extract the meaning of the long sentences and make it comprehensible to them. Those who write textbooks don't always have a great deal of consideration for second language learners!

So, have students make a list of complete subjects, from their readings. Play with changing adjectives, prepositional phrases, appositives, and clauses. Once they create these new subjects here are some things they can do with them:

1. Verbalize them as tongue twisters.
2. Verbalize them with various strong emotions.
3. Have contests to choose the best performances.
4. Post the unique colorful subjects on the bulletin board
5. Have them locate and pronominalize the simple subject.

FOR EXAMPLE:

The sample sentence below could be from an academic reading:

*A Nobel prize winning internationally acclaimed **researcher**, a woman in her late forties, from Harvard University which is doing in-depth research on 3-D biological printing*

This example can be played with to become any number of monster phrases. Let students play with their monsters. There is no need for truth or accuracy just convert the academic sample into a funny monster/s:

1. *An internationally acclaimed **singer**, a promising female rock **star** from Las Vegas, whose performance is impersonating the best singers from the sixties = (SHE)*

2. *Some long legged creepy **spiders**, hairy creatures, from sandstone caves in Australia, whose survival strategy is to nest in people's ears and lay their eggs = (THEY)*

3. *The hilarious freckled-faced young **boy**, a red head elementary kid, from the nearby town that manufactures air balloons = (HE)*

4. *That electrically automated stainless steel **robot**, the small android, that wears black leather vests from the designer who won the prize for the best fashion creator in the world = (IT)*

Long subjects from academic readings provide great templates. Advanced students can rewrite them by using their right brain and adding interesting vocabulary. The new vocabulary provides a rich bonus.

When the long subjects are finished and ready. They should be pronominalized according to the accordion principle. For maximum right brain acquisition, the following can be done with the subjects:

THEY CAN BE REPEATED WITH:

Scorn

Envy

Amusement

Incredulousness

Anger

Indignation

Fear

Horror

Foreboding

THEY CAN BE READ:

Slowly

Quickly

Whispered in secret

Screamed

Stuttered

Mumbled

THEY CAN BE FRAMED AND DISPLAYED:

On poster boards

On the wall

In a collective 'monster subject' book

Illustrated by students

Labeled—'*Famous Subjects*'

After finding the simple subject, it will be easy to pronominalize it. And as a reminder, the two important reasons for doing this are:

1. By isolating the complete subject, you mark the end of S, in SVO. This means your 'noun phrase' (first brother) is dressed in full costume, has all his make-up on and is ready to do his job: carry the prima donna (verb/phrase) on stage for the star performance of the evening!

2. The pronominalizing process simplifies the subject so it can correctly stage its performance with the verb (subject verb agreement). They can now dance together in harmony! After all the subject and verb are the indispensable parts of a sentence. They give the core performance. Like a well-rehearsed dance routine, they have to be in step with each other.

S and V are the heart and soul of every sentence or clause.
Without them we have no show!

ACHIEVEMENTS AND PITFALLS

ACHIEVEMENTS

First and second person pronouns (I/YOU/WE) used as subjects are almost always unadorned. As such they are the beginning and the end of the complete subject. This makes it easy to match the verb that follows them. There is not a lot you can add to them.

They are very valuable pronouns however and are used almost exclusively in oral conversation or dialogues. *The Great Pronoun Giveaway* activity is an excellent practice for this reason.

On the other hand, the adjectives, phrases, appositives and clauses we used in the *Wildest Subjects Activity* focused more on the rest of the pronouns (HE/SHE/IT/THEY). It was not only done for the purpose of creating long and interesting subjects but also to practice the third person pronouns when the accordion finally closed up again!

Between the two activities we covered essentials for SVO and
'How to think in English'

PITFALLS

Pronominalization can be tricky. Locating or defining the simple subject gets harder the longer the noun phrase. If students have practiced in the early stages they will be ready to tackle longer noun phrases when they come to academic writings. Some tricky knots along the road are the following:

GENDERLESS SUBJECTS:

In the example below, the simple subject, **acrobat** does not give us a clue about its gender. The pronoun cannot be IT, unless the acrobat is an animal or robot. So, we must assume the acrobat is HE or SHE:

*The spectacular world famous **acrobat** from Cirque du Soleil whose skill is demonstrated at high altitudes and depicted in precarious angles*

Structurally it doesn't matter if it is HE, SHE or IT. All three will use the same verb. But if you can clarify the gender, you can continue referring to that subject by its proper gender when substituting it with a pronoun. Adding an appositive is one way of doing this.

*The spectacular world famous **acrobat** from Cirque du Soleil, **a young woman in her mid-twenties**, whose skill is demonstrated at high altitudes and depicted in precarious angles IS SPEAKING TO REPROTERS IN **HER** DRESSING ROOM BACKSTAGE.*

CLAUSES:

Pinpointing the simple subject can be difficult because of clauses which often include verb forms or nouns. This can be very confusing for students if they don't know the requirements for correct verb tenses. Clauses are particularly difficult because they may have omissions shown as follows:

The **man** wearing the black leather boots

*The **man*** (S)
Wearing the black leather boots (Clause describing which man)

When students see 'wearing' they may think 'the man' is the complete subject and wearing is the beginning of the verb phrase. Wearing, however cannot be the verb because there is no 'is' to make it a progressive tense.

Wearing is part of a clause that has omitted words. A native speaker has verb tenses and omissions internalized, but a learner does not.

The omission is shown below and if we add it, the learner will understand that it is a clause describing the subject. Clauses like this can have the omitted words added for students initially. It would be comparable to adding training wheels on a bike.

The **man** [WHO IS] wearing the black leather boots.

*The **man*** (S)
who is wearing the black leather boots (dependent clause, describing which man)

Because even easy clauses have subject and or verb components, they should to be practiced during the early part of learning to avoid confusion later on.

I believe [that] putting the omitted word in brackets helps students. The 'training wheels' will not usually be there at higher levels.

Check here for more <u>examples and mini quiz</u> (Hyperlink in Bibliography).

What a blessing that you have played the accordion with all this already!

HOW TO THINK IN ENGLISH SUMMARY

CHECK LIST FOR THE SVO COMPONENTS:

SUBJECT:

Sentences or dependent clauses start with a noun (phrase).

Noun phrases can be a proper name, a pronoun or a long noun phrase.

Noun phrases also follow quite a strict word order.

Noun phrases with singular nouns start with a determiner to determine the noun.

Plural noun phrases may not need a determiner if they are universal.

Proper nouns or pronouns do not need a determiner but may have an appositive.

Subject nouns and phrases are pronominalized with (I/you/he/she/it/we/they).

Subjects can be preceded or started with extra information (how/when/where/why).

For foundation students, it is best to put the additional information at the end.

VERB:

Verb phrases starts immediately after the complete subject and include all types of verbs, simple present, simple past and all other verb tenses created with regular, common, special, transitive, intransitive, linking, phrasal verbs etc. These will be covered in detail in my upcoming book.

OBJECTS:

Transitive verbs almost always require a direct object.

Transitive verbs may also have an indirect object.

Objects must come after the verb, hence SVO.

Objects can be pronominalized with (me/you/him/her/it/us/them).

Linking verbs do not take objects but may take an adjective compliment.

Linking verbs do not take objects but may take a noun compliment.

Linking verbs do not take objects but may have added information (how/when/where/why).

Intransitive verbs can take compliments (optional)

Any sentence may have a compliment with added information (how/when/where/why)

These compliments are best put at the end but can come before the subject.

NOTES:

S and V are always necessary (in that order) and accountable for a complete sentence.

Only imperative sentences have no visible S because YOU is their subject, and it is understood. YOU is left out to differentiate between a statement and an order. An order can only be given to the listener: YOU

The O is only inseparable and accountable in SVO when it comes after SV in the form of an object of the verb action (transitive verbs).

The verb phrase itself is the hub of the sentence so the type of verb dictates whether it needs an object, a compliment or nothing!

YOU and IT are the same, both as subject or object, so placement is crucial. We know if they are sender or receiver according to what side of the fence (verb) they are on—before or after.

Noun phrases, whether they come before or after the verb, still follow the rules of noun phrases. A noun is a noun is a noun whether it is subject, object, or even the object of a preposition. See the section: *You 'Gotta' Nail Down the Noun.*

Linking verbs are intransitive, this includes: BE (all forms): AM, IS, ARE, WAS, WERE, WILL BE, WAS BEING, and HAS BEEN. Other intransitive verbs include, appear, become, feel, look, seem, smell, sound, taste.

If BE leads the verb phrase in simple past or present we know it is not transitive because BE cannot take an object since it is a linking verb. You can HIT someone but you can't BE them.

NOTE:

BE is the only linking verb in English that can form a partnership with a transitive verb. The partnership (progressive) involves: BE, + transitive verb + ING.

If the companion verb is transitive it can then take an object. You cannot really say: She was pizza, but you can say: She was eating pizza (was + eat + ING).

Otherwise BE is a copula which means the subject will in some manner be equal to something else. Think of BE as a measuring scale or an equal sign between two things:

She = nice
It = a beetle
We = tired
They = neighbors
Clothes = new

Finally, I hope this book on How to Think in English was useful to you. It is my aim to help teachers understand the structure of English from the bottom up. Thinking in the language is the first step.

If you would like to read weekly articles with valuable ESL/EFL tips, sign up to receive them in your email. Also, feel free to check out our webpage for more resources: www.leonawellington.com

GLOSSARY

Adjective: a word that helps describe a noun (person place or thing)

Adverb: a word that tells more about the verb or action in the sentence

Appositive: A phrase that follows the subject, can represent or substitute it and is set off by commas.

Dependent Clause: a partial sentence that cannot stand alone. It has a subject and verb that do not function alone. For more examples and a quiz click here. (Hyperlink in Bibliography).

Determiner: a word that initiates (determines) a noun or noun phrase

Direct Object: the object being acted upon by a transitive verb

ESL: English as a Second Language is when English is taught to speakers of other languages in a country where English is the spoken or native language

EFL: English as a Foreign Language is when English is taught to people in a country where English is NOT the spoken or native language

Indirect Object: the person or object receiving the direct object

Intransitive Verb: a verb that does not take an object

Linking Verb: a verb that does not take an object but links the subject to some quality or thing

Noun: a person place or thing

Object Pronouns: me/you/him/her/it/us/them

Preposition: a word that starts a phrase and has an object (noun)

SVO: the word order of English: Subject/Verb/Object

Subject Pronouns: I/you/he/she/it/we/they

Subject: the main author or initiator which comes in first position in a sentence or clause

Transitive verb: a verb that requires an object

Verb: action or state of being carried out by the subject (comes in second position, after the subject)

ABOUT THE AUTHOR

Leona did not always want to be a teacher. In fact, she preferred fine arts and travel. But she did always have a keen desire to help others. Growing up in Southwestern USA, of Hispanic heritage on her mother's side, she knew what it felt like to be at a disadvantage.

So, when she had the opportunity to teach English in a village in Costa Rica, it was her chance to help brilliant, deserving students succeed, despite their scant resources and lack of access to private schools and social opportunities.

With a BA (Secondary Ed), a Master's degree in education (M.Ed.-TESL) And a Cambridge International Diploma for Teachers and Trainers (CIDTT) UK, Leona has traveled to different parts of the world teaching ESL/EFL and doing consulting and teacher training in Costa Rica, Oman, Kazakhstan, and Sweden.

Leona is particularly interested in helping teachers who are often overburdened, underpaid and lack opportunities for professional development, especially when laboring in remote areas. She knows that these teachers make a huge difference in the lives of countless students so helping even one teacher at a time can exponentially help multitudes.

She believes that learning a language should be exciting and fun, not difficult or intimidating. Students should never have to live in fear of letting their parents down because they failed to fulfill their parents' scholastic dreams or missed opportunities for jobs, careers and scholarships.

Creativity and intelligence are abundant among
all students even in the remotest areas

By providing tools, content, tips and methodologies to help teachers, she hopes to help more students. It's also a way of protecting the Lingua Franca for worldwide communication, which in turn will help facilitate peace, understanding, and mutual cooperation among nations.

Learning English should be built on a solid foundation that covers the core building blocks of the language. The aim of this book is to help both beginning and advanced students get back to basics by encouraging them to think in English. Doing so will facilitate correct growth as they advance. To contact Leona, visit her website: www.leonawellington.com

DEDICATION

This book is dedicated to...

...all the talented and brilliant students who want to get ahead but live in remote areas and lack opportunities

...native English speakers who are not trained in linguistics or the mechanics of their own language and yet find themselves teaching to speakers of other languages in order to meet the huge demand for English around the world.

...all ESL/EFL teachers who are striving to give their students the best possible start in the language so they can compete at higher levels

...the millions of ESL/EFL students attempting to enter an elite global community where the endless stream of knowledge and information is constantly updating and outdoing itself.

...my grandchildren and other children around the world who are now being raised with multiple languages, without understanding the mechanics of any of them, yet mastering them all before even starting school.

…all children of the world who hold the secret to acquisition, and are experts in acquiring any language simply by being in it.

...all those who strive for world communication and peace through one dependable language they can use worldwide.

...www.pixabay.com whose awesome graphics breathe life into the text and make writing and reading so much more fun

...Christina Hills and https://websitecreationworkshop.com/ for the awesome instruction in helping me create my own WordPress website without being a techie and after two webmaster failures:
www.leonawellington.com

BIBLIOGRAPHY

Books/Seminars:

Brinton, L. J. (2000). *The Structure of Modern English: A Linguistic Introduction*. Philadelphia, PA: John Benjamins, North America.

Han, Z. (2004). *Fossilization in Adult Second Language Acquisition*. Tonawanda, NY: Multilingual Matters, Ltd.

Mahler, M. (2005) *Seminar in Applied Linguistics*, Framingham State University, Costa Rica, Overseas Extension Program

Websites:

Lawler, J. (2017). *Must appositives be in the same person?* <English.stackexchange.com> Retrieved 7 April 2018, from https://english.stackexchange.com/questions/376236/must-appositives-be-in-the-same-person

Simmons, R. (1997-2018). *Grammar Bytes!: The Appositive.* <Chompchomp.com> Retrieved April 4, 2018 from http://www.chompchomp.com/terms/appositive.htm

Simmons, R.L. (1997-2018). *The intransitive verb; recognize an intransitive verb when you see one.* Grammar Bytes. Retrieved May 6, 2018 from http://www.chompchomp.com/terms/intransitiveverb.htm

Simmons, R.L. (1997-2018). *The transitive verb; recognize a transitive verb when you see one.* Grammar Bytes. Retrieved, May 6, 2018 from http://www.chompchomp.com/terms/transitiveverb.htm

Shrives, C. (2028) *Clauses / what are clauses*: Grammar-monster.com Retrieved, May 6, 2018 from http://www.grammar-monster.com/glossary/clause.htm

Nash, K. (2018) *Linking verbs: English grammar 101 lesson 3 module 3 verbs*. Laguna Niguel CA Cingletree Learning. Retrieved May 06, 2018 from https://www.englishgrammar101.com/module-3/verbs/lesson-3/linking-verbs

www.ingramcontent.com/pod-product-compliance
Lightning Source LLC
Chambersburg PA
CBHW060952040426
42445CB00011B/1122